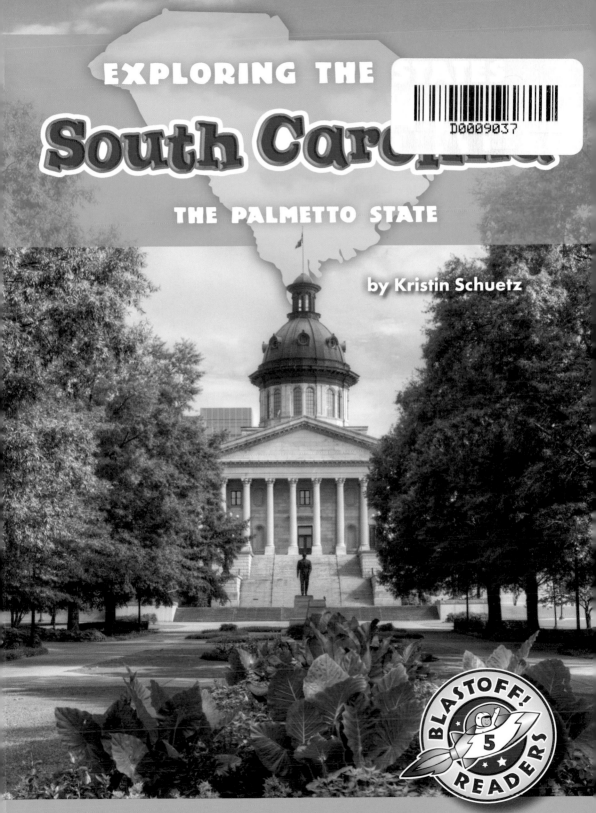

EXPLORING THE

South Carolina

THE PALMETTO STATE

by Kristin Schuetz

BLASTOFF! READERS
5

BELLWETHER MEDIA • MINNEAPOLIS, MN

Note to Librarians, Teachers, and Parents:

Blastoff! Readers are carefully developed by literacy experts and combine standards-based content with developmentally appropriate text.

Level 1 provides the most support through repetition of high-frequency words, light text, predictable sentence patterns, and strong visual support.

Level 2 offers early readers a bit more challenge through varied simple sentences, increased text load, and less repetition of high-frequency words.

Level 3 advances early-fluent readers toward fluency through increased text and concept load, less reliance on visuals, longer sentences, and more literary language.

Level 4 builds reading stamina by providing more text per page, increased use of punctuation, greater variation in sentence patterns, and increasingly challenging vocabulary.

Level 5 encourages children to move from "learning to read" to "reading to learn" by providing even more text, varied writing styles, and less familiar topics.

Whichever book is right for your reader, Blastoff! Readers are the perfect books to build confidence and encourage a love of reading that will last a lifetime!

This edition first published in 2014 by Bellwether Media, Inc.

No part of this publication may be reproduced in whole or in part without written permission of the publisher. For information regarding permission, write to Bellwether Media, Inc., Attention: Permissions Department, 5357 Penn Avenue South, Minneapolis, MN 55419.

Library of Congress Cataloging-in-Publication Data

Schuetz, Kristin.
 South Carolina / by Kristin Schuetz.
   pages cm. – (Blastoff! readers. Exploring the states)
 Includes bibliographical references and index.
 Summary: "Developed by literacy experts for students in grades three through seven, this book introduces young readers to the geography and culture of South Carolina"–Provided by publisher.
 ISBN 978-1-62617-040-7 (hardcover : alk. paper)
 1. South Carolina–Juvenile literature. I. Title.
 F269.3.S38 2013
 975.7–dc23
                                                                 2013014946

Printed in the United States of America, North Mankato, MN.

Table of Contents

Where Is South Carolina?

South Carolina is a triangular state in the southeastern United States. It covers an area of 31,114 square miles (80,585 square kilometers). North Carolina meets South Carolina's northern border. The Blue Ridge Mountains are on the northwestern edge. To the west of South Carolina is Georgia. Columbia, the state capital, sits in the center of the state.

Sandy sea islands dot the Atlantic Ocean to the east of South Carolina. The **Intracoastal** Waterway lies between the mainland and these islands. It is a major shipping route for states on the East Coast.

North Carolina

Rock Hill ●

● Greenville

South Carolina

Columbia

★

Congaree
National Park

North Charleston ●
● Mount Pleasant
Charleston

Georgia

Atlantic Ocean

N

W ● E

S

South Carolina was one of the thirteen original **colonies**. Many historic battles of the **Revolutionary War** were fought in the state. Before settlers arrived, **Native** Americans lived on the land. **Slaves** arrived in large numbers when cotton became a major crop in the South. In 1860, South Carolina left the United States to form the **Confederacy** with other slave states. The southern Confederate states fought the northern Union states during the **Civil War**.

Civil War

South Carolina Timeline!

1670: The English build the first permanent settlement in the Carolina colony. It is named Charles Towne after King Charles II.

1729: North and South Carolina become separate colonies.

1776: South Carolina and the other original colonies declare independence from Great Britain. The British do not recognize their freedom until the Revolutionary War ends in 1783.

1788: South Carolina becomes the eighth state.

1860: South Carolina leaves the United States to form the Confederacy.

1861: A battle at Fort Sumter begins the Civil War.

1868: South Carolina rejoins the United States.

1900s: Textile mills move to the state from the north and provide jobs.

1922: The boll weevil and drought destroy the cotton crop.

1989: Hurricane Hugo hits South Carolina after reaching wind speeds faster than 155 miles (249 kilometers) per hour!

Battle of Fort Sumter

Hurricane Hugo

Revolutionary War

Blue Ridge Range

South Carolina's Climate

average °F

spring
Low: 51°
High: 74°

summer
Low: 69°
High: 89°

fall
Low: 53°
High: 75°

winter
Low: 35°
High: 57°

South Carolina's landscapes rise from east to west. The highest land is in the northwest Blue Ridge Range of the Appalachian Mountains. Sassafras Mountain, the highest point in the state, is located in this rocky region. The Piedmont **Plateau** meets the mountainous west. Rolling hills stretch across this part of the state. Scattered **monadnocks** stick out of the land.

Coastal **plains** cover eastern South Carolina. The inner plains are made up of forests and sand hills. The outer plains are flat with rivers and swamps. The Pee Dee, Santee, and Savannah Rivers travel east through the plains. They empty into the Atlantic Ocean.

fun fact

More than 60 miles of beaches line the eastern coast of South Carolina. This strip is called the Grand Strand.

Congaree National Park

Trees in South Carolina's Congaree National Park form one of the world's highest **canopies**. There are towering pines and giant cypresses. The forest sits in central South Carolina on the Congaree River **floodplain**. During times of flooding, many of Congaree's animals climb the tall trees to find dry escapes.

cypress knees

Unique formations known as cypress knees grow above the roots of cypress trees. They look like dwarves next to the tall tree trunks. Oxbows are scattered throughout the park. These U-shaped lakes are old river bends that are no longer part of a river's course.

Wildlife

South Carolina's thick pine forests are home to white-tailed deer, opossums, black bears, and southern fox squirrels. Red-cockaded woodpeckers live in the holes of old pine trees. Spotted salamanders hide in wet soil under rocks and logs.

Brown pelicans and American oystercatchers hunt on the Atlantic coast. The oversized beak of the pelican is designed to scoop up fish. The oystercatcher uses its long, narrow beak to pry open shellfish. Loggerhead sea turtles lay their eggs on South Carolina's sandy beaches. Hatched baby turtles crawl across the sand to join dolphins and right whales in the sea.

American oystercatcher

spotted salamander

loggerhead sea turtle

wild hogs

Landmarks

Angel Oak Tree

Sites in South Carolina give visitors a glimpse into the nation's past. People can take a boat ride to an important Civil War site in Charleston Harbor. **Fort** Sumter is where the first shots of the war were fired. Middleton Place and Drayton Hall are old **plantations** that are home to beautiful mansions and gardens.

Lower Whitewater Falls

Drayton Hall

Fort Sumter

There are also many natural wonders to see in South Carolina. Angel Oak Tree on John's Island shades more than 17,000 square feet (1,579 square meters). The tree is estimated to be hundreds, or even a thousand, years old! Near the North Carolina border, Lower Whitewater Falls drops 200 feet (61 meters). It is one of the most visited waterfalls in the Blue Ridge Mountains.

Charleston

Charleston is South Carolina's oldest city. In 1670, English settlers made it the first permanent settlement in South Carolina. At that time it was located just across the Ashley River. Visitors to Charleston can step back in time to experience colonial life at Charles Towne Landing. They can also walk The Battery by the harbor. This stretch was once a defensive seawall.

Today, Charleston is the second largest city in South Carolina and an important **seaport**. Cargo ships and cruise ships travel through the harbor. The city also has an appreciation for the arts. The Gibbes Museum of Art displays more than 10,000 works of art. Just a few blocks away, the city orchestra performs often.

Gibbes Museum of Art

fun fact

Charleston is famous for its azaleas. Many visitors come to catch a glimpse of their red, pink, white, and purple blooms.

The Battery

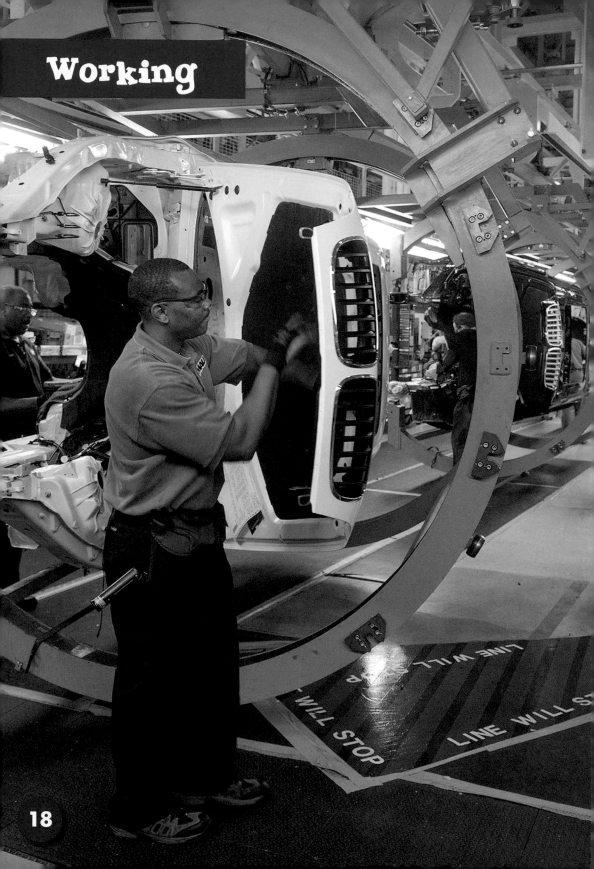

Working

South Carolina's warm climate and coastal location are ideal for farming and fishing. Important crops include cotton, soybeans, tobacco, and peaches. Chickens and cattle are also raised on farms. Fishers catch shrimp, crabs, clams, and oysters from the Atlantic Ocean. Loggers cut down trees from South Carolina's large forests to use for lumber and paper.

Manufacturing provides jobs for many South Carolinians. They make cars, chemicals, and other products in factories. **Service jobs** are also an important source of work for people in South Carolina. Some people work for banks, schools, and hospitals. Others help the **tourists** who come to learn about the state's history or relax on the beach.

Where People Work in South Carolina

manufacturing
10%

farming and natural resources
2%

government
15%

services
73%

Myrtle Beach

South Carolina's coastal **resorts** on Myrtle Beach and Hilton Head Island attract tourists year-round. Visitors relax on sandy beaches and play tennis and golf. Campers, hikers, and canoeists head to Congaree National Park and the state's other wild areas. On the Chattooga River, kayakers and whitewater rafters battle the currents.

kayaking the
Chattooga River

Clemson Tigers

Sports fans cheer on college teams like the Clemson Tigers
and the South Carolina Gamecocks. They also root for
minor league teams such as the Charleston Battery soccer
team. Competitive bass fishing tournaments draw many
people to lakes around the state.

Sweet Potato Pie

Ingredients:

1/3 cup butter, softened

1/2 cup sugar

2 eggs, lightly beaten

3/4 cup evaporated milk

2 cups mashed sweet potatoes

1 teaspoon vanilla extract

1/2 teaspoon ground cinnamon

1/2 teaspoon ground nutmeg

1/4 teaspoon salt

1 unbaked pie shell (9 inches)

Directions:

1. In a bowl, cream butter and sugar. Add eggs and mix well.

2. Mix in milk, sweet potatoes, vanilla, cinnamon, nutmeg, and salt.

3. Pour into pie shell. Bake at 425°F for 15 minutes.

4. Reduce heat to 350°F. Bake an additional 35 to 40 minutes or until a knife inserted near the center comes out clean.

5. Cool. Store in refrigerator.

6. Top with whipped cream.

chitlins

barbecue pork

Like the rest of the South, South Carolina is a place to enjoy comfort food. A mushy corn mixture called grits is a common food in the state. Barbecue pork is a favorite main dish. Meals that feature seafood are also popular. She-crab soup is a creamy chowder made with the orange eggs of female crab. Frogmore stew is a collection of shrimp, corn, sausage, and potatoes.

On warm days, South Carolinians refresh themselves with a glass of sweetened iced tea. Sweet potato pie and peach cobbler satisfy cravings for sweets. Unique snack foods include boiled peanuts and benne wafers. Benne wafers are thin cookies covered with sesame seeds.

World Grits Festival

Many of South Carolina's festivals celebrate food. The World Grits Festival is a three-day event in Saint George. People at the festival compete in a rolling-in-the-grits contest. They have a limited amount of time to get grits stuck to their bodies. The Chitlin Strut in Salley every November has a hog-calling contest. In coastal cities, visitors eat up at seafood festivals.

Arts gatherings draw huge crowds, too. The Spoleto Festival in Charleston is an arts event that happens every spring. It offers 17 days of performances by actors, musicians, and dancers. Bluegrass music festivals are also popular.

! fun fact

Reenactments of famous battles from the Revolutionary and Civil Wars transport South Carolinians back in time.

The Gullah

A unique group of African Americans has survived in South Carolina's coastal areas and sea islands. The Gullah are **descendants** of slaves who were brought to work on rice plantations. When slavery ended, the freed slaves lived **isolated** lives on the sea islands. This helped them to hold on to their culture and lifestyle.

Making grass baskets and fishing nets by hand are important parts of the Gullah culture. They share history through storytelling and singing. Spoken **folktales** usually bring animals to life with expressive voices and faces. **Spirituals** tell about times in slavery. The Gullah are a living example of the preserved history in South Carolina.

Fast Facts About South Carolina

South Carolina's Flag

South Carolina's flag is packed with symbols of the Revolutionary War. The blue background matches the color of the colonist soldiers' uniforms. The crescent is borrowed from the soldiers' hats. The palmetto tree represents a successful defense against a British attack.

State Flower
yellow jessamine

State Nickname:	Palmetto State
State Mottoes:	*Animis Opibusque Parati*; "Prepared In Mind and Resources"
	Dum Spiro Spero; "While I Breathe, I Hope"
Year of Statehood:	1788
Capital City:	Columbia
Other Major Cities:	Charleston, North Charleston, Mount Pleasant, Rock Hill, Greenville
Population:	4,625,364 (2010)
Area:	31,114 square miles (80,585 square kilometers); South Carolina is the 40th largest state.
Major Industries:	farming, fishing, manufacturing, services, tourism
Natural Resources:	forests, waterpower
State Government:	124 representatives; 46 senators
Federal Government:	7 representatives; 2 senators
Electoral Votes:	9

State Bird
Carolina wren

State Animal
white-tailed deer

Glossary

canopies—thick coverings of leafy branches formed by the tops of trees

Civil War—a war between the northern (Union) and southern (Confederate) states that lasted from 1861 to 1865

colonies—territories settled and ruled by people from another country

Confederacy—the group of southern states in America that formed a new country in 1860; the Confederacy fought against the northern states during the Civil War.

descendants—those related to a people group of the past

floodplain—a plain that is often underwater

folktales—stories that are handed down from one generation to the next

fort—a strong building made to protect lands

intracoastal—within coastal waters

isolated—set apart and alone

manufacturing—the business of making goods from basic materials

monadnocks—isolated, steep hills

native—originally from a specific place

plains—large areas of flat land

plantations—large farms that grow coffee, cotton, or other crops; plantations are mainly found in warm climates.

plateau—an area of flat, raised land

resorts—vacation spots that offer entertainment, recreation, and relaxation

Revolutionary War—the war between 1775 and 1783 in which the United States fought for independence from Great Britain

seaport—a harbor for ships

service jobs—jobs that perform tasks for people or businesses

slaves—people who are considered property; African Americans were bought and sold as slaves in the Southern United States until the late 1800s.

spirituals—religious folk songs

tourists—people who travel to visit another place

To Learn More

AT THE LIBRARY
Burgan, Michael. *Fort Sumter*. Minneapolis, Minn.:
Compass Point Books, 2006.

Jerome, Kate Boehm. *South Carolina: What's So
Great About This State?* Charleston, S.C.: Arcadia
Pub., 2008.

Raven, Margot Theis. *Circle Unbroken: The Story
of a Basket and Its People*. New York, N.Y.: Farrar,
Straus and Giroux, 2004.

ON THE WEB
Learning more about
South Carolina is
as easy as 1, 2, 3.

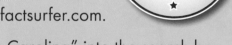

1. Go to www.factsurfer.com.

2. Enter "South Carolina" into the search box.

3. Click the "Surf" button and you will see a list of
   related Web sites.

With factsurfer.com, finding more information is just
a click away.

Index

The images in this book are reproduced through the courtesy of: Sean Pavone/ Dreamstime.com, front cover (bottom); (Collection)/ Prints & Photographs Division/ Library of Congress, p. 6; Antonio Abrignani, p. 7 (left); North Wind Picture Archives/ Alamy, p. 7 (middle); NOAA/ Satellite and Information Service, p. 7 (right); Daveallenphoto/ Dreamstime.com, pp. 8-9; windjunkie, p. 9; Natalia Bratslavsky, pp. 10-11; Pierre Leclerc, pp. 11, 14-15; visceralimage, p. 12 (top); Marek R. Swadzba, p. 12 (middle); Benjamin Albiach Galan, p. 12 (bottom); IbajaUsap, pp. 12-13; Bob Downing/ MCT/ Newscom, p. 15 (top); Owaki-Kulia/ Corbis, p. 15 (middle); Blaine Harrington III/ Alamy, p. 15 (bottom); James Schwabel/ Age Fotostock/ SuperStock, p. 16 (top); Dave Allen Photography, p. 16 (bottom); ClimberJAK, pp. 16-17; Bloomberg/ Contributor/ Getty Images, p. 18; Associated Press/ The Island Packet, Jay Karr, p. 19; StacieStauffSmith Photos, pp. 20-21; Wayne Hughes/ Alamy, p. 21 (top); Associated Press/ Tom Priddy/Four Seam Images, p. 21 (bottom); msheldrake, p. 22; genky, p. 23 (top); David P. Smith, p. 23 (bottom); Richard Ellis/ Alamy, pp. 24, 26-27, 27 (bottom); Kevin M. McCarthy, p. 25; Associated Press/ Layne Bailey, p. 27 (top); Pakmor, p. 28 (top); Kenpei, p. 28 (bottom); Glenn Price, p. 29 (left); Tony Campbell, p. 29 (right).